The Gospel of Barbecue

Wick Poetry First Book Series

The
Gospel
of
Barbecue

Poems by

Honorée Fanonne Jeffers

The Kent State University Press

Kent, Ohio, and London

07 06 05   5 4 3 2

The Wick Poetry First Book Series is sponsored by the Stan and Tom Wick Poetry
Program and the Department of English at Kent State University.

Library of Congress Cataloging-in-Publication Data
Jeffers, Honorée Fanonne 1967–
    The gospel of barbecue / by Honorée Fanonne Jeffers.
        p.   cm.—(Wick poetry first book series)
    ISBN 0-87338-673-6 (pbk.: alk paper) ∞
    1. Afro-Americans—Poetry.   I. Title.   II. Series.
PS3560.E365 G6   2000
811'.6—dc21   00-032728

British Library Cataloging-in-Publication data are available.

For Mama, love always through good, bad, and memory

and

For Mr. Ray Grant, the first person to call me a poet

Contents

Acknowledgments

Grateful acknowledgment goes to the magazines and anthologies in which these poems first appeared, some in earlier versions: "Only the Yellow" and "The Light Brigade," *African American Review;* "To Keep From Shouting Something," *Beyond the Frontier: Black Writing at the Millennium;* "Wynton Marsalis Plays in Buckhead (Atlanta 2/2/92)," *Brilliant Corners: A Journal of Jazz and Literature;* "I Was Looking at Miles," *Catch the Fire!!!: A Cross-Generational Anthology of African American Poetry;* "Philly in the Light," *Callaloo;* "Poem For Me and Mine," "My Mother's Memories ('Now My Mother Will Remember')," and "The Gospel of Barbecue," *Cave Canem;* "The Two Graces" and "To Touch God," *Crab Orchard Review;* "The Beautiful Saturdays" and "Useless Things," *Crack;* [I Cannot Write a Poem to] Bless All the Givers of Pain," *Identity Lessons: Contemporary Writing About Learning to be American;* "I have Dreams of My Father," "Mary Don't Weep," "Missing Tolstoy," and "Swing Low, Sweet Chariot," *Obsidian II;* "Big Mama Thornton," "Eyes of Soon Children," "Memphis Resurrection," *Poet Lore.*

Gratitude first and foremost to the Creator from Whom all life and words descend; to the Ancestors for providing me with the gift of remembrance, especially Charlie James and Lance Jeffers; to Trellie James Jeffers, Alvester James, Thedwron and Marie James, Edna James Hagan, Florence James Shields, Charles James, Marcus Todd Searcy, Valjeanne Jeffers Thompson, and Sidonie Jeffers; to Mrs. Queen Ester Culp, Mrs. Yokely, Mrs. Barbara Cook, Jerry Ward Jr., Hank Lazer, Myron Tuman, Harold Weber, and Karla Frye; to dear friends Ifeoma Nwankwo, Heidi Durrow, Shreerekha Pillai, Kavita Sharma, Josi Pastora, Kimberly Clark, Andrea Franckowiak, Mae Garcia Williams, Erika Smith, Mary E. Weems, Aishah Shahidah Simmons, Carlos and DeSonuia Wise, Lori Amy, and Yvonne Jackson; to Cave Canem, especially Toi Derricotte, Cornelius Eady, Sarah Micklem, Father Francis Gargani, Elizabeth Alexander, Michael Harper, Afaa Michael Weaver, Sonia Sanchez, Herman Beavers, Hayes Davis, Lyrae Van Clief-Stefanon, James Richardson Jr., Vincent Woodard, Rachel Harding, John Frazier, John Keene, Lenard D. Moore, and Yona Harvey; to Maggie Anderson, Christine Brooks, and Erin Holman at The Kent State University Press for making this book come together and for all their hours of hard work treating my book as if it were their own; to Michael Collier and the Bread Loaf Writers Conference; to Quincy Troupe and the "Write Now" Summer Workshop of Cleveland, Ohio; to the colonies and foundations that generously supported me through the writing of this book: the Rona Jaffe Foundation for Women Writers, the Hedgebrook Colony, the MacDowell Colony, and the Barbara Deming Memorial Fund for Women.

And so many thanks to Ms. Lucille Clifton for picking my manuscript for the Stan and Tom Wick Poetry Prize and for her own glorious poetry.

So I give you all my right hand of fellowship and love, and hope for the same from you. . . . Maybe all of you who do not have the good fortune to meet or meet again, in this world, will meet at a barbecue.

—Zora Neale Hurston, *Dust Tracks on a Road*

The Gospel of Barbecue

2000

I

Will meet
@ the BBQ

Tuscaloosa: Riversong

for Mister Weaver

1. *Black Warrior speaks*

The night before they came,
I walked on my river. I had strange
dreams: bloody shouts to the sun,
bodies in the trees, twirling legless.
I sang until morning. I sang, and the white
ones were here sniffing an empty breast.
They are here but I cannot die.
My tribe is strong behind our
drums and sliced trees.
We are strong against these whites
with sticks like dirty breath, these
silly children snatching toys.
They do not see me.
My tongue is strong and hides me.
I cannot die. They do not see me
walking on my river, my teeth biting
at early chains. They only
know they choke on my songs.

2. *DeSoto speaks*

I have seen him before all
over the world. This Indian,
this Tuscaloosa, this red man
with the black name dares
to think he will defeat me
and my tribe. Who is he to imagine
he will kill me with his songs,
sacred or commonplace?

3

Who is he to be sure that his spirits
will hear, float down this river,
sting the skin of slaves?
I am the one who cries the music
of God, and Tuscaloosa is mine.
He cannot live past my morning
into night. I want his seed to die
in this water. I want his mouth
wounded with slime.

Tuscaloosa.
I will push him into that river,
this warrior of a cracked womb.
His song will never be earth or flesh.

3.

Tuscaloosa sleeps in the water
stirs the silt of blues
makes music of ashes
feeds death clotted anger

Tuscaloosa sleeps in the water
sucks gore from his lungs
strips the green crucifix
roars the gumbo scream

Tuscaloosa
Tuscaloosa
Tuscaloosa

Coltrane

Trane's *Alabama*
a Creole agony
blood slung through air
a throat-filled epiphany
death licking madness
an elegy for mud

> *angry*

4.

This is the river of no longer.
Here by the side of the Black Warrior,
lights are woven through branches.
Water level signs hang from the trees:
1919 1857 1913 1989 and on.
A memory of what is no longer
painful. From year to year
the levels of the water climb
higher than before, and in the spring
the people of the town visit
mounds filled with bones.
They buy feathers and skin painted
bright colors, or whistles drilled
with holes that make sounds
of animals unnecessary and small.

No one talks of the year he died.
Tuscaloosa is a river, a place
where quiet blood is shed.
Tuscaloosa is a river, signs
nailed to trees. We do not speak
in old tongues. We blow pretty
noises through holes.

5

5.

Tuscaloosa
This is not the river, so long,
so wide, Hayden's water, baptism
of survival. The river that Mama
and I crossed over one summer,
crossed over history's concrete
back, the river that made her ask,
Do you think we should pray I can't
see the shore this is the river the slaves
had to cross oh God I can't see
the shore do you think we should pray?
This is not Jordan, only the river
DeSoto tossed three hundred souls into,
watched the water grow tall
as they squirmed like dancing
stones, watched the water dark
and struggling rise and rise,
bubbles blowing from the children's
mouths, mother's wet chants
swallowed by dirt.
This is not Jordan.
There is no milk and honey
waiting on the other side, only
dead stones flat and smooth.
This is not Jordan, only simple water
muddied from a season of rain.
This is not Jordan, but I have
prayed at this shore anyway.

6

6.

Tuscaloosa
feathered with spirit
red libation on the tongue
claws mystery into earth
scatters song on this river

Tuscaloosa
prayer of ancient thirst
wind through clenched fist
claws mystery into earth
scatters song on this river

Tuscaloosa
holy man swept into light
gnarled root of God
claws mystery into earth
scatters song on this river

Tuscaloosa
Tuscaloosa
Tuscaloosa

dark arms cup the blade
blue spit in the scripture's eye
do not walk across my water
do this in remembrance of me

24 hours

II

Ellen Craft

I keep reminding my husband that we both ride
to Freedom. Mine is a temporary pretense
but he clearly sees that it is wonderful
for anyone to be Master if only for a fortnight.
If only for one hour.
Even as William jokes that he is my slave
until we leave this train, he glares
beneath my man's hat and clothes,
my suddenly pale ways. My skin
and my husband's pen are our passports
into Jordan—William knows this and still
he watches me. He wonders if I will leave him
once I step onto Northern land and take
off this natural mockery, change into what others
would have me be. Or worse, stay to celebrate
our trickery when all our lives I shall
stare at him with the eyes of a white man.

"Chapel Hill, N.C.
Oct 19th 1861

Master:

    All is well but Lucy. She is about but not
very well. I am sory that I did not have the opportunity of writing
sooner. I have a bad chance to write. Business is dull. I am just
able to live. I have no young men to wait upon and can get
into no very profitable business. If times was like they have
been I could have earned good wages. I have done all I could.
If you are satisfied please let your humble slave know, so
that I can make farther arrangements. I lost about half my
last sessions wages. When the war broke out the students
volunteered and did not pay me for my labor.
My youngest child is able to sit alone. My wife has generaly
kept up pretty well. Provisions is very high.
Please let me know how all are. I remain your faithful obedient
an humble slave. Jerry Hooper.

Give my love to all."

The Gospel of Barbecue

for Alvester James

Long after it was
necessary, Uncle
Vess ate the leavings
off the hog, doused
them with vinegar sauce.
He ate chewy abominations.
Then came high pressure.
Then came the little pills.
Then came the doctor
who stole Vess's second
sight, the predication
of pig's blood every
fourth Sunday.
Then came the stillness
of barn earth, no more
trembling at his step.
Then came the end
of the rib, but before
his eyes clouded,
Uncle Vess wrote
down the gospel
of barbecue.

Chapter one:
Somebody got to die
with something at some
time or another.

Chapter two:
Don't ever trust
white folk to cook
your meat until
it's done to the bone.

Chapter three:
December is the best
time for hog killing.
The meat won't
spoil as quick.
Screams and blood
freeze over before
they hit the air.

Chapter four, Verse one:
Great Grandma Mandy
used to say food
you was whipped
for tasted the best.

Chapter four, Verse two:
Old Master knew to lock
the ham bacon chops
away quick or the slaves
would rob him blind.
He knew a padlock
to the smokehouse
was best to prevent
stealing, but even the
sorriest of slaves would

risk a beating for a full
belly. So Christmas time
he give his nasty
leftovers to the well
behaved. The head ears
snout tail fatback
chitlins feet ribs balls.
He thought gratitude
made a good seasoning.

Chapter five:
Unclean means dirty
means filthy means
underwear worn too
long in summertime heat.
Perfectly good food
can't be no sin.
Maybe the little
bit of meat on ribs
makes for lean eating.
Maybe the pink flesh
is tasteless until you add
onions garlic black
pepper tomatoes
soured apple cider
but survival ain't never been
no crime against nature
or Maker. See, stay alive
in the meantime, laugh
a little harder. Go on
and gnaw that bone clean.

[handwritten margin notes: "sic!"; "Stay alive in the meantime laugh a little harder"; "Maker"]

Music, Buzzing of Absence

A cow's going to need her tail more than one fly time.
—African American Proverb

Where did you drive me?
Can't see a soul
here in my lonely
field. No calm pat
or *there, there*
locates my cries.
Hair spinning on end,
fingers scraping
the bloody itch.
Music, buzzing
of absence.
Where is the silk,
the air when my skin
flickers, water now
that I remember thirst?

Eyes of Soon Children

How does my father
look, my father who is not
yet my father? Does he wear
his thick halo of hair?
Can he be my father
when he is thin and alive?
It is fifty years ago in
a San Francisco restaurant.
My father's waiting for the cousin
he's never met, who passes
as a white man. A white man
who rides on trolleys unafraid,
tips a hat at even whiter ladies
who could fall and stay
in love with him in an hour.

My father squints, tries
to spot his cousin. He makes
up excuses for his own
strangeness in this room.
Before he leaves, finally seeing
that no one will ever show,
only this comforts him:
he would have known
his cousin by the dark eyes
of his soon children,
the eyes that betray
and name him as one of us.

*passes
as a white man*

Only the Yellow

A child cannot be like a poem.
My mother assures me of this.
She says you cannot throw a child
away like a word in a poem.
Like *dark,* though my grandmother
did this to my mother.
Grandma looked at my newborn
mother and wanted to place her back
in the womb where God forgives darkness.
My mother: too dark for my barely
brown Grandma, for Grandma's yellow family
who thought they were the chosen ones.
My mother: too dark to bring to church
where the people looked at Grandma
and her dark baby and smiled to themselves.
Vengeance be to God.

I wonder if Grandma saw all this the day
my mother was born:
Did she see my mother at six, the dark patch
over my mother's eye, the eye gone to a butcher knife?
Did Grandma see that my mother
would grow up to hate her?
Did Grandma see that my mother
would grow up to love her dark self?
Did Grandma see my mother headed for places
beyond Putnam County, Georgia,
where only stuttering Willie Molton (the murderer
of words) would want her?
Did Grandma see that it was a lie that only
the yellow will know the face of God?

Now My Mother Will Remember

She first fell in love with my father's
poems, *I was wearing a blue chemise*
and he made up a verse right there
on the spot. Those words were verbal
foreplay. She jokes only now that he is dead,
long after I needed faded images.
Mother, father, meeting of my familiars.
Light and dark against each other.
Long after I found it harder to believe
she loved a man robbed of his bared teeth.

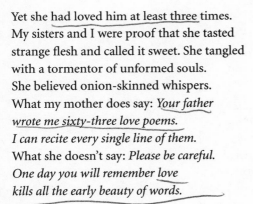

Yet she had loved him at least three times.
My sisters and I were proof that she tasted
strange flesh and called it sweet. She tangled
with a tormentor of unformed souls.
She believed onion-skinned whispers.
What my mother does say: *Your father*
wrote me sixty-three love poems.
I can recite every single line of them.
What she doesn't say: *Please be careful.*
One day you will remember love
kills all the early beauty of words.

the beautiful saturdays

for christine

don't go outside
your hair will go back
grandma pleaded
threatened   you danced
in puddles   laughed
laughed   your teeth
fierce   laughed   she beat
you laughed   skipped
screamed in the rain
and then a miracle
of your rusty wire

Nice!

the saturday smell
of burnt pomade
i would beg to be
straightened but with me
there was no transforming
the bad into good   you tried
anyway   touched my face
combed and plaited
my thin hair

before your temples
were anointed with burns
before your eyes
closed against me
before you slid a needle
like love into your flesh
you roared at the rain

you held me between
your knees   braided my
hair in a million patient rows
you made me beautiful
when your fingers
crowned my head

21

To Keep from Shouting Something

for Butch, Val, and Sisi

1. *Arkansas circa 1910*

rules for
right of way
step off
the curb
for a white
man woman
child don't
try to be brave
or play tightrope
walk along
the sidewalk
edge tiptoe
or teeter
perform for
the audience
the faces
flushed
in triumph
the sidewalk
is conquered
manifest
destiny

2. *Nebraska circa 1917*

This is what happens when you forget
the right of way:
Your wife strengthened by age, never
how you would have her,

confused brown eyes caught in brightness.
Your wife packing bags for the West,
brow unwrinkled, calm.
Your wife holding a gun on a white mob coming
to remind you that black always means step aside,
but you are hiding under the floorboards.
Your wife's knuckles big and rough
and ready to pull the trigger.
Your wife lacking the softness of white women,
the true measure of feminine love.
White men turning their horses
around in the road, feeling sorry
and ashamed for her husband.

3. Nebraska circa 1929

The first wife, the black wife, my father's
grandmother, sits to the side of the casket
at the grave sight. Today she is burying
the black doctor who has not been her husband
for over ten years now, the black doctor
who left her for a white woman.
The first wife watches the white wife
sitting right in front by the hole in the ground,
and the first wife concentrates on dirt
dropping on top of the doctor's coffin.
She thinks of the land now lost to her,
of the man she is sure this white woman
killed before he can be reclaimed,
and she knows she should keep her gloved
hands folded in her lap.
She should remember the ceremonies
of the middle-class. Instead, she starts

screaming. She becomes very colored.
She is not ashamed.

4.

Maybe you think all this is a simple
story and you assume who told
me and why. My father, of course.
My father who hated what he understood
too well. What would you say if you knew
that all my childhood I had seen pictures
of a white woman in our album, initials
M. E. F., holding my smiling two-year-old father,
his legs short and fat and rounded in an O?
After my father's death my mother
showed me the picture of another woman,
a five-foot-two woman who had held a gun
on a mob of Ku Klux Klansmen to protect
her black husband. A nameless woman with kinky
hair piled on top of her head, her thick lips
pursed tightly to keep from shouting something.

My father didn't speak to me about this
black woman, only the white one.
He said this white woman was the kindest
woman on earth. She kept him from freezing
to death one winter in Lincoln.
Her neck was fragrant and she sang
in an alto voice. My mother says this
white woman was a good nurse,
one who knew all the right poisons
that caused a black man to forget
what he was or made him die trying.

Bless All the Givers of Pain

Prose Poem

for Toi Derricotte

I cannot write a poem to bless all the givers of pain a poem to forgive those who should not be forgiven a poem to go on forever that starts with my grandmother who gave birth to my father through pain into pain my grandmother who loved and hated my father my grand-mother who gave her only child away my grandmother who told my father she wished he didn't have nappy hair so he wouldn't be a nigger my grandmother who ignored my sisters and me my grandmother who kept pictures of my dark sister and me in her photo album my grandmother who kept pictures of my fair sister up on her mantle my grandmother who called me three times in twenty-four years my grandmother who called me dear my grandmother who died without telling me she needed me my grandmother who gave birth to my fa-ther who married my mother whose mother gave birth to her through pain into pain my grandmother who hated and loved my mother my grandmother who called my mother black and ugly my grandmother who called me pretty and brown my grandmother who was ashamed of my mother my grandmother who was proud of me my grand-mother who would not believe my mother my grandmother who is crazy and will not recognize my mother anymore my grandmother who gave birth to my mother who gave birth to me through pain into pain my mother who gave me her milk in exchange for my silence my mother who would not believe me or herself my mother whose words I hold in my mouth my mother who loved me who loved me who loved my father who loved my mother who hated my father who hated my mother who married my father who loved and hated me my father who gave me his poems through his seed my father whose face is worn by every man who raped me my father who claims me as his child when I am no longer his child my father who frightens me when I don't have to be afraid of him my father who hit me with his hands my father who held me to his heart that deserved to explode in the pieces that I keep in my fingers to write this poem for the givers of pain who I hated who I loved who made me ugly who made me beautiful

25

Cut Stalk of Hydrangeas

for Solomon

The big pink
baby's head
pushing out
surely hurt
the earth.
The cut means
cradle theft,
long days
of loss and
milk frothing
on petals.
These wide
leaves might
nurse forever
here without
swaying in air
or leaning
toward songs
poured back into
garden crust.

Swing Low, Sweet Chariot

And they thought we were
talking about heaven.
After all, we had not studied
the masters' poesy, we knew
nothing about central metaphors,
conceits, literary vehicles.
Chariots carrying us home
on the underground railroad.
No, we were picking cotton
or tobacco or peaches and glorifying
tragedy with our voices.
We were weeping bitter, large tears.

Mary Don't You Weep

They sing of Mary and Martha,
the sisters of Lazarus.
O Mary don't you weep
O Martha don't you moan
They sing of the slave woman
who birthed thirteen children,
by a slave master who tells her every year,
You can keep this one,
and every year he forces
her to give up a baby
whose small, blind mouth seeks
emptiness and the slave
woman cannot cry aloud
for fear of her master.
They sing of Pharaoh's army
that got drowned in the Red Sea,
Pharaoh's army of slave masters
who chased Moses into the jaws
of the Promised Land,
and they sing of retribution,
of the soldiers in the water
who are sucking blood
like rivers of milk
and Lazarus arises
from the tomb, shakes dust
from his flesh and cries,
Yes, I proclaim!

Feast of Saint Agatha

for Miss Sonia

1.

The governor of Sicily
sends me silk. I stroke
the cloth, look in the tiny
holes between the threads.
Everyday God sends
come letters from this
Lord Quintian scented
with incense: *Cast off*
these fetters, walk
to me. I promise
life beyond walls.
The man lies I know,
but paper tastes
good on my tongue.
I chew while I pray.
My ring finger itches.

2.

Quintian's notes
grow more frequent,
his smell chases
me around my room.
I want him.
He strokes my
ugliness, he sucks
my breath in sleep.

I want him but
Jesus stuffs his fist
between my legs.

3.

If I cannot hide
behind the rock
then make me worthy.
Thou hast taken
me from the love
of the world, given
me patience instead.
Thou seest my heart,
thou knowest my
desires. Do Thou
alone possess me.
Thou hast owned
me from the cradle.
I am Thy sheep.

4.

These are my shackles:
I am plain.
I am pure.
I am sanctified.
Sometimes in my cell
at night I hear Jesus
speaking in Quintian's
voice, stoking
the red center
of my flesh. I grow

weird

bread in place
of these troublesome
arcs that draw sin.
He calls me
to squat water
on fire. I turn
my eyes inward,
fill my mouth
with feathers.
He calls me.
My arms float
upward, my lips
cut stigmata
in gold palms.

III

Big Mama Thornton

They call me Big Mama and I make
much music when I walk. I know
you want to find the easy way
down to these marrow-full bones,
but please don't mess me over.
Don't play me like a puppy, lick
my face then bark at me. Do
and the two-headed lady gone
have your address and your
unlisted phone number.

I weigh three hundred pounds
and all this is real, baby. Ain't
nobody else living with me in this plush
house of mine. This just some deep
country meat padding your ride.

They call me Big Mama and the ground
be strumming stones.
These fine hamhocks will knock
your black iron pot all night long
but please don't mess me over.
Don't play me like a puppy, lick
my face then bark at me. Do
and I'll cut you so smooth,
I'll be on that train to Chicago
before you even start to bleed.

Memphis Resurrection

> Who died and made you Elvis?
> —Bumper sticker

The big rock by my door
is a plaster prop, after
all. I'm back to hear
screams for what I can't
do, couldn't do forty
years ago. Awkward
pelvic thrusts fooled
the camera and virgins,
but I have no more fish-
fry tunes left to dress
up on brand new plates.
This time around,
I spend all day singing
cracked Mississippi
homilies. Why
did I want to live
forever in the first place?
Salvation felt better dead,
floating home free
while my bones, secret
and brown, mingle
with old dirt.

The Lady Esu-Elegbara Finally Speaks Out

for Vincent

These people won't recognize
me. They stand right
outside the temple door
but decline to come in, keep
their gifts to themselves,
and always ask when my
Papa will be back home.

What's with them giving
me messages to take upstairs
like I'm some secretary blowing
smoke in their faces?

I must confess I get a
little ugly on occasion.
I give them curses with my
blessings, send my made-up
songs to the sky.

Being a woman sometimes
is good. I can always blame
Daddy, *Ah, men! Do they
ever hear your prayers?* I say
I wrote down just what I
heard them ask for. I say
there's no subtlety with divinity.

Take what comes their way
or leave it but outrage
gets them no refunds.

What do they want from
me anyway? If they bothered
to look, they could see who
I've been the whole time.

I am Papa. Papa is me.
The impatient stone
beneath this dress goes
way beyond drag.

Bop: To Know You Is to Love You

for Grandma Florence

I need to find me a lover before I get
grateful, and come a time when nobody
will start or keep with me. When I'm looking
to the Sunday road for a man too poor
to be handsome, too old to matter. Walking
through rain, wearing salvation brogans.

To know you is to love you
But to know me is not that way it seems

Before too long I'll be wanting something
I can't name, settle instead for one swollen
belly after another, no time to flatten
before that bigging brush come sweeping
my way again. Babies and my new blood,
babies and my cracked nipples, babies
sitting on my kitchen floor, sucking
hungry thumbs, looking my way.

To know you is to love you
But to know me is not that way it seems

I'm gone find me somebody, anybody to really
love before I smell like old fatback and greens,
before my last choice dies on me and all them
babies get grown, leave me to the grease
on my stove. Before the roaches take over
my mind and I fall asleep to their scuttling.

To know you is to love you
But to know me is not that way it seems

On Listening to the Two-Headed Lady Blow Her Horn

She don't sing high
    and can't scat worth

a damn either but
    she breathes roots

into all manner of things.
    Have you hopping

like a toad frog
    into your next life.

All manner of things.
    Yes—rain and thunder.

All that but you
    ain't prayed in so

long. Why bother
    with fancy now?

Once you found out
    who God was it

ain't good to you
    no more. I know.

Loving any woman
    is such hard work.

Uh-huh. Tough.
    See her moving down

that mother of pearl,
     the mute trailing

bones? There it
     is. Now listen:

the *duende* wind.

azure ella

day gone. miss ella,
blue woman, pipes moon rapture.
slow pathos ascends.

dusty scat drifts, plucks
mood lit cadences. *lonesome,*
i'm so, so lonesome.

insistent dark grace
lifts, flies across soprano
madness assembling.

sparrowed oracle
moaning lost-time harmony,
trebled dream praises.

can't see. stringed night tongue
croons azure suffering. gone
millennium song.

Secondhand Blues

for Emeka

A Memphis cliché: my first
visit and you insisted

I hear the real blues,
indigo forecasts,

broken glass syrup.
I said we never can be sure

the blues is authentic
since we all borrow pain

from someplace, never
give it back. I wanted

jazz instead but blushed
when you asked, *Is alto*

sax your favorite horn?
We took the long

way to Beale Street,
parked on some road.

By the time you finished
singing your sweet, imitation

woe, I was real ready
for firsthand blues.

Beale Street was empty,
lonely for music.

I Was Looking at Miles

Keith, the white man
who lived next door, invited
me over to see Miles Davis
on the color TV & then Keith
started talking in the middle
of *Autumn Leaves.*
Keith read in a medical journal
that black men really are bigger
but does size matter?
Miles was on that horn,
his face fracturing in ecstasy.
Should I tell Keith that I don't hold
a thing against pale men or their bodies?
I don't think I am racist. At least,
I am not politically opposed
to loving. I wondered if I should
be nice to Keith who was providing
me with more than one night's worth
of entertainment, but I was looking
at Miles when I told Keith that I couldn't love
a man who couldn't make me blow a note
as sweet & high as Miles just did.

Useless Things

> I am requesting that all of you join me in constant prayer, that in
> the name of Jesus, God will deliver our mother from the strong
> hold of Satan regarding her fear of people and spells.
> —From Uncle Thed's letter to the family, June 8, 1998

My mother's mother turns her head sometimes.
Other times she undoes the buttons
on her blouse. Fingers quick,
she holds the flat breasts inside,
believes they aren't soft, useless things.
She points out her wedding picture,
two people beyond me who wear heavy
clothes with small buttons to confuse
the fingers. She wants to give me
a chance to escape. *Look at me and Charlie.*
I wasn't nothing but a child then.

Sixty years of petrified youth hang
over spattered fly swats, Cheeto bags,
right across from the gossip window
facing an old, empty house: her now
dead husband, his black skin
refusing to shine; her now insane
smile breakable as a blue china vase
wrapped in tissue. I know I look
just like her but no, that isn't me.
See her on the wall, eyes squinting
where mine are wide?
See her sitting on her ragged sofa
now, wrinkled as I will never be,
track of white going up the middle
of her hair?

She lost her mind in degrees
after Charlie died, a dream becoming
cloudy in the morning.
I have no husband to drive me crazy,
but I know one day I will see into
the sinful hearts of passersby, yell
at them to be ashamed.
The very legs they walk on are defiled.
The men are dogs, the children thieves.
Of course, every woman is a whore.

The Two Graces

At school, I was nothing and special
at the same time, the only black girl
in the sixth grade and the only non-Catholic.
My mother was a Primitive Baptist turned
more decorous A.M.E. Methodist,
and my father was one of the two black
atheists in the world. The Sister Graces
at St. Thomas More tried hard to advise me:
Perhaps your mother could do something about
your hair. You know, Jesus forgives
all sins, even those one inherits.

The Sisters would wait each Friday outside
of confessional while I tried to confide in Father Dan
(*I had impure thoughts and actions—but Daddy*
says masturbation is normal. Okay, then, Charlie Wong,
Edgar Fineberg, and I drank five cups
each of Mogen David at the Our Jewish
Friends' Passover Celebration).
I wanted to ask about the blood in my underpants.
Could I still be saved?
I thought of the two Graces, the bleak coifs
pressing lines into the sides of their faces,
and I refused to name my need.

Confessions of the Colored Left at St. Thomas More School

for Yvonne, Josi, and Kavita

Edgar Fineberg, Charlie Wong, and I were tight.
We were ridiculous enough to define
ourselves, though not one of us was white or Catholic.
We got drunk on Kosher Passover wine
Fineberg brought from home, and we talked real loud.
We whispered, *Fuck you, fuck you,* at Sister Grace's
back when we knew she could pray us into hell.
We laughed in the back of Church during school Easter
Mass while Father Dan peered over the tops of his half glasses:
*Who are the punks who dare to giggle at the Blessed
Wounds of Our Lord Jesus Christ?*
We weren't afraid. He couldn't threaten us with God.

Poem for Me and Mine

me me me

> Is it because we bleed so regularly that everyone thinks we are
> supposed to?
> —Pearl Cleage, *Deals with the Devil and Other Reasons to Riot*

Can we please just
admit/for the sake
of argument/that I am
being raped

or beaten or killed
& left on the streets

or by the side of I-20

or on the floor of my
brand new cobalt kitchen
I had my architect copy
from *Martha Stewart
Living*

Maybe you're thinking
that I shouldn't be
outside at four
A.M. anyway

I should be indoors
looking at the moon
& the stars through
my curtained window

I shouldn't be sleeping
in my own house
alone either

Solitude is such
a bourgeois illusion
& community should
be on my mind
all the time even when I
am screaming but I don't
know how to save us both

I only have one survival
map printed on the inside
of my right eyelid & I'm
thinking about whether
we can exist at the same time

How can I keep you
from exploding/hide from
a bullet coming through
you at me but first
try to catch
your guts flying off
in the other direction

Haven't I sucked
my air in secret

Haven't I leaned
into a fist / a false
promise

Haven't I swallowed
the barrels of guns

50

Haven't I wanted
so badly for them
to taste sweet

Haven't I slept
on needles piled
on nails

Haven't I opened
my legs with a smile

This is the lie

I am less than you
You are because I am
not / I don't get tired
of making sure you always
stand taller when we
are both crawling
through piles
of our dead

Here's the truth

The social scientists still
call me / after three decades
& two & one half
movements / *the oppressive
black matriarch* / &
they are right

I plan to be a tyrant
just as soon as I ask
you for permission

drink muddy water

this man.
this man make love's
fingers speak in glory.
this man make me see inside
my flesh like jesus
wave his hands.
this man.
this.
man.
make me say i won't
when I know next time
coming right back around.
him.
i won't. say i won't.
no next
time. no. say i won't
(i want / say it again / i want / want).
make it rain in this place.
make me bless his air.
make my throat dry
and i lick ash sweet.
yes.
i'm ready now.
gone sleep in that hollow
log just for this man.
grab my spoon. get
to digging.
got my cup in the mud
just for this man.

IV

Down Home Blues

I don't know
why my man
wants to fight.
I played him fair.
The day before
we said *I do*
I told him,
I like my blues.
I like my liquor.
In that order.
If you want to hit
the streets with me
we can dance
all night. If you
don't, expect me
in the morning.

hold it steady

on the one: the same
minimalist row
to hoe. a black man
cowskin sweats on the side
of a dirt road. screams.
his obsessive conk
goes back to an afro.
back again.

baby
baby
baby
    baby
    baby
    baby
        baby
        baby
        baby

this is an in-pocket work song.
hold it steady while I hit it.
(justonce)
do you reckon that's getting it?
(thenoncemore)
no machine quick tapping
just the sucking of that same
sweet plain beat.

on the one: stripmining
the syncretic
hole / the doors opening
like your nose.

what's my name?
you know my mama
didn't call me that.

say grace. then fry up this urban
fatback sweeter than butter.
psychotic
      black-eyed peas
on the side.
for
dessert you can have my cakes
& eat them too.

hold it steady
baby
baby
baby
hold it steady
(umph / thenoncemore)
hold it steady while i hit it
all the way
        home.
you take
the bottom.

The Truth of It

I slept in my bed in daylight;
at night, looked for God in my closet.
At night, my father rode my soul, a Legba
with crooked knees, fat cigar in mouth.
My father was back from the grave
and spoke in jumbled tongues.
My father was a puppy nibbling
my face and hands, leaving
behind inky streaks.
My father was crazy, crazy, crazy
for jazz, danced the jitterbug (with rhythm
this time), hummed *Flying Home*.

After one dream, I turned on all
the lamps in the house. I hedged my bets,
prayed while lists ticked in my head:
I needed to get an oil change.
I needed groceries (rice and beans,
milk I couldn't drink).
My altar was just a Bible, some candles,
picture of Mary and Jesus plucked
from my childhood. The truth of it
was only voices washing over me,
a blanket of second skin.

Dreams of My Father

Or a man who looks like him.
I only know I call him *Daddy*
(as all southern women
do until the day we die).
In my dreams he is still alive
and this is not a comfort.
I am my best when tragic.
Grief becomes me.
Daddy is more real in death,
eyes dark, undimmed
by the grave, smile less sincere.
Matter clings to his thick
eyebrows, his mouth spits mud
when he tries to talk. He is candid.
He tells me he liked my sisters better than me.
Most times I search for him in a crowd
of counterfeit Daddies.
I look for pieces of him.
An elbow. Black hair on the back
of a pale neck. If I find him,
I will say, *Is that you?*
I know you this time.

southern women

59

Where the Song Stops

These walls of yellow.
These easy drops
of blood.

I can't go nowhere
without running
into myself.

I've got it bad
and that's
where the song
           stops.

Not even
split knuckle love.

Not even
the sweetness
of a hiss.

Why can't I get one
note's blessing?

Every night howling
at this sorry moon
like it's some big
           surprise.

Not even
the scavenger's
rhythm.

Not even the good
blues, a logic
of warning.

Houses just fall
right down in front
of me.

A twisted rope hangs,
calls out any
body's
      name.

Ezekiel Saw de Wheel

> And when the living creatures went, the wheels went by them:
> and when the living creatures were lifted up from the earth, the
> wheels were lifted up.
> —Ezekiel 1:19

Poor Ezekiel, what
a lonely man.
Feel sorry for him:
who cares to notice
Ezekiel's cracked brow,
his holy frowns?
No one says he's the one.
i saw   i saw
the spirit entered me
i saw four wheels
four wings   loins circled
by fire   dogs licked
the honeyed blood
of jerusalem
i saw   i saw
quickly fall down
swallow the dust
Who cares if he knows
mountains speak,
sees man, lion, ox,
eagle peeking
out of the open
side of the Lord?
i saw   i saw
way up
in the middle
of the air

in the middle
in the middle
in the middle
in the middle
in the middle
in the middle
Prophet or no prophet,
anyone who talks
to God is crazy.

7

An Old Lady Told Me

An old lady told me, *Every real woman*
has a rape fantasy at least once in her life.
I refuse to believe her. I'm a real woman.
I've never had a rape fantasy.
I've never imagined *they come at night*
myself tied to a four post bed with Hermés
silk scarves, the ones with little appropriate
they come to hurt us they come riding symbols
all over them while a faceless *they called our names*
man bends above me, his narrow hips pointed
right *they were our neighbors* at my brain.
I know that old lady thinks I dream of power,
of giving it up to someone else or having it stolen
and having that feel good. She thinks I want
distance, but where is the part about blood and fists,
my gargling with gasoline a million times?
Or the scene where *they knew our names*
they took hurt us hurt us we tried to be modest
we tried I scratch his name *to hide ourselves*
to cover on a public bathroom wall *our heads*
with sheets they hurt us we ran when the bullets
started the paint slicing off *they buried my daughter*
as easily as my skin *by the trees over there*?

The Light Brigade

In college, we used to call
them *the light brigade*,
that cluster of girls with skin
no darker than sandpaper.
There were four of them:
The fat one who looked at my dark
mother, her English professor,
as if Mama had no right to be living.
The one whose room
smelled of cooked hair grease.
The one with the rich parents
who sent her ten dollars every year.
The one with no parents.
They reminded me of the strange
soup I read about once in a children's book.
The little-bit-of-everything soup.
Carrots, cabbage, meat, and stones.
A trickery stew.

We called them what we did to keep
from hissing *high yellow* through our teeth.
High yellow. I can say that out loud now.
If I can't heal the sick, I do know the disease.
They weren't really yellow anyway.
They were some indefinable color,
something we longed to name but could not.
Not yellow, the color of my mother's kitchen.
Not cream, the color of my mother's palms.
Not gold, the color of my mother's thin
wedding band she gave me when my father died.
We did not say *high yellow* then.

We were strivers.
We compared ourselves to these girls,
our walking light brown paper bags.
We were silent, too dark to claim
honesty as our privilege.

Wynton Marsalis Plays in Buckhead (Atlanta 2/2/92)

for Ray Grant

He's wearing the trademark
Really Nice Suit, but the fingers
have yet to play that clickety-
clack rapid tune he's been famous
for since Julliard. Of course,
the crowd is not happy & in a minute,
they might want their money back.
Not much church up in here
except for a sprinkling of dark
voices so he starts playing a New Orleans
funeral chant to us, stops every third
beat or so to let the few moan in the salty
spaces. Right in the middle of Miss
Daisy's back yard, Wynton smuggled a small
fuss in the pocket of that tailored suit—a sneaky
Amen clamp on his trumpet.
I know jaybird talk can be loud & secret.
I know to wake up in the morning before buzzards get to work.
I know all the words to this funky
death song when Wynton's fingers finally
move into that contentious blur the others
want so badly. The white man on my left
snorts, *It's about time somebody started
playing some music,* falls immediately into a real
trance, doesn't know the day I was born there
was a riot & meanwhile I was waiting
for some kind of commotion.

To Touch God

The women of Flat Rock
Church, my Grandma's Sisters:
darker and stranger
than the nuns at my school.
I used to love to see
a Flat Rock Sister catch
her Spirit. Sweat flowed
from under her wig.
Her body shuddered. Arms
and legs opened to thank Jesus.
When she shouted, I longed
to lay my small hands on her
and touch God rising in waves
from her wrinkled black skin.

sunday dinner

for robert

you stole plums right from mister
henry love's front yard
lived with all those brothers
and sisters in a four room house
dropped out in eleventh grade

surely you were headed to jail
like your brother eddie serving
life for helping to sodomize
mutilate a white girl one
night leaving her for dead
on county line road

eddie in prison every sunday
evening your mama not ashamed
cooked fried chicken and biscuits
eddie ignored your mama and dinner
talked with you about his last real
piece was good even if he and junior
had to take it from her

eddie ignored your mama started
crying when eddie said he should
hang himself like junior after dinner
one sunday evening pulled
down by the belt buckle

your mama said she sure
was glad lord knows
she was glad junior went out like
that only after he and eddie
shared a good sunday meal

69

i am your courtier

for mama

a fourth sunday
deacon i kneel to wash
your feet   rough antiqued
worn yellowed ivory
you are a child rising in cold
or rain or baked heat   your heels
bare and patient on the clay
i paint you with colors
richer than the memory
of cruel earth

Missing Tolstoy

for Daddy

> The Tostolyans   the Afro-American slaves
> knew this: you could be killed
> for teaching people to read and write
> —Adrienne Rich, *Your Native Land, Your Life*

Who at twelve years old can know
the mysteries of Anna Karenina?
Who needs to know? Of course, now I wish
I had not destroyed Anna the Christmas
you gave her to me, ripped her pages out one
by one because she wasn't Judy Blume.
And I wish I had not walked out in the middle
of your Sunday Tolstoy readings, that you
hadn't called after me, *Please wait. Listen.*
You're the only one of your sisters
who'll hear the pathos of these lines.

I hated your Russians who lived in death,
and you loved what no one wanted to remember:
the nickname you called me (*little brown baby*),
the self-absorbed suffering, the woman
named Anna I did not know I would become.
It is only now that I can piece together
the pages of tragedy, dig in earth and shape
the words with your mouth.

Philly in the Light

for Hayes

Y'all carry weapons up here
in the grocery stores? I ask
the security guard at the corner
SuperFresh. He's bagging fruit for me,
and there's a gun on his hip. If I
weren't such a Southern Belle,
I'd say right to his face, *That's a mighty*
big piece you're carrying. I'd make my voice
deliberately corn pone and molasses
and he'd laugh, charmed by my
ignorance of the Great Migration pace.

I am an Eve in this northern garden
where trash planted one night
sprouts ghettos the next morning.
Where they dropped fire on a whole
city block, watched the chickens, goats,
people burn all day long on television.
They smelled cooking flesh
in the air and called it barbecue.
I shake my head at these city dwellers
who don't know that killing should
be done in private, never for open
eyes or in the light.
This is a lesson that even the children
of the South have learned.

Bitter

72

Prayer for Flat Rock

Hmmmmhmmmm
We calling on you Jesus
We calling out your name
We calling on you Jesus
We calling on your word

Church
This is the time for water
pouring on feet
dirt turning to hunger
scripture cutting into skin
Old prayers stop
here on Flat Rock
Old prayers lay
on their hands

Hmmmmhmmmm

And there are birds
speaking in blood

You been so good to me Lord

And there are mouths
drinking death gourds

You been so good to me

And there are shrouds
sewn for the earth

Hmmmmhmmmm

Church
This is the time for carving
God from stone
for digging up graves
and kissing bones
Roots been working
here on this Rock
Flat Rock been
tugging at my soul

74

TUSCA — WARRIORS
Lusa — Black

found poem

Notes

"Tuscaloosa: Riversong" gets its name from two Creek or Choctaw words, *tusca* (warriors) and *lusa* (black). In 1540, Chief Tuscaloosa battled the Spanish explorer DeSoto at Mauville, Alabama, 100 miles north of modern day Mobile. Chief Tuscaloosa and his entire tribe are assumed to have died in that battle. Today, a city in Alabama as well as a river (Black Warrior) is named for Tuscaloosa.

"Ellen Craft" retells the story of a very fair-skinned African American woman, Ellen Craft, and her husband, William, who escaped from slavery by disguising themselves as a young white gentleman and his body servant who were traveling from Georgia to Pennsylvania. Ellen disguised her feminine appearance by cutting her long hair and swaddling her face in a cloth because of "toothache pain." Since Ellen could not read, she also pretended to have an injured hand; William, who was literate, signed all papers for his "master."

"[Master / All is well but Lucy.]" is a found poem, taken from the John Berniere Hooper Papers in the Southern Historical Collection, University of North Carolina at Chapel Hill.

"The Feast of Saint Agatha." In A.D. 251, Quintian, the governor of Sicily, tried to force Agatha to live with him. When she refused, he had her arrested as a Christian, tortured her and cut off her breasts. An earthquake occurred while she was being tortured; fearing the people would rise against him, Quintian stopped the torture of Agatha. Her injuries were too severe, however, and she died soon after. The Holy Roman Catholic Church later canonized Agatha.

"Big Mama Thornton," a figure of early rock and roll/rhythm and blues, was the original singer of "Hound Dog," a tune later covered and made famous by Elvis Presley.

"The Lady Esu-Elegbara Finally Speaks Out." The divine Yoruba trickster interprets the wishes of humans to the gods. Esu sometimes is depicted as one dual-gendered figure that has full breasts and an eternally erect penis. In the "New World," Esu is often called "Legba" or "Papa La Bas," an old man who smokes a cigar and limps.

A "two-headed lady" is someone with great spiritual powers who works magic or voodoo on others. She may also be able to see into the future.

"To Touch God." Flat Rock was a very large, table-like stone approximately ten feet across. It rested in a creek in Putnam County, Georgia, and was a Native American holy site. About a hundred yards from the creek was a Primitive Baptist Church named for the Rock. A few years ago, the stone was dug up from the creek, but Flat Rock Church still stands and the people still come to worship.

GEORGIA

The Church still stands